A Woman With
Childhood Issues

MIN. DEBREA HOWARD

A Woman With Childhood Issues
Debrea Howard

© September 2019 by Debrea Howard

All rights reserved worldwide. This book is protected by the copyright laws of the United States of America.

No part of this publication may be reproduced, distributed, or transmitted in any form or by any means, including photocopying, recording, or other electronic or mechanical methods, without the prior written permission of the publisher, except in the case of brief quotations embodied in critical reviews and certain other noncommercial uses permitted by copyright law. For permission requests, write to the publisher, addressed "Attention: Permissions Coordinator," at the address below.

Scripture quotations are taken from THE HOLY BIBLE, NEW INTERNATIONAL VERSION®, NIV® and/or King James Version, KJV

Published by Pecan Tree Publishing
October 2019
Hollywood, FL
www.pecantreebooks.com
adminservices@pecantreebooks.com

978-1-7341058-2-7 Paperback
978-1-7341058-3-4 Digital
Library of Congress Control Number: 2019915215

Cover and Interior Design by: Charlyn Samson

Pecan Tree Publishing
www.pecantreebooks.com

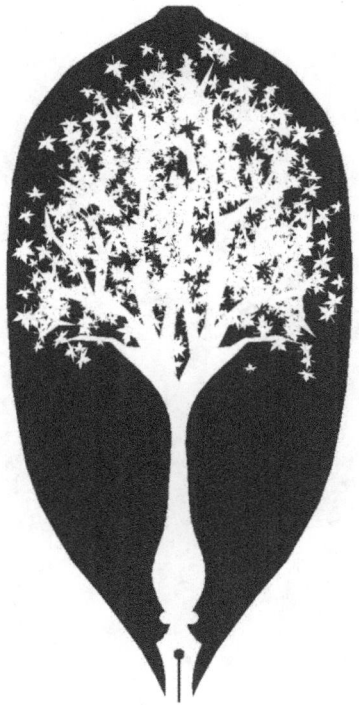

New Voices | New Styles | New Vision –
Creating a New Legacy of Dynamic Authors and Titles
Hollywood, FL

Dedication

I dedicate my life and this book to my Lord and Savior Jesus Christ; without Him, I am certain I would not be here to share this story with you.

I dedicate this book to my three children: Kesha, Joy and Terell.

Thank you for being patient with me through all the ups and downs of life.

When you read your mom's story here, hopefully you will look back and understand some things better.

Your love means the world to me.

Much love, Mom

Acknowledgements

First, I would like to thank my Mother, Ezalia Clark for all your patience, dedication, unconditional love; and the years of prayer you have prayed on my behalf. Mom, you never gave up on me even when I wanted to give up on myself. You've always told me the truth and have proven to me that God's love and forgiveness are real. Because of you, that love, and forgiveness are a powerful part of my life. I will forever be grateful to you. I would not be the woman I am today without your love and prayers. May God continue to bless and keep you in His care. I love you very much!

To my sister Vera, sis, words cannot express the love and respect I have for you. You have been there for me through thick and thin. There were times I didn't know if I was going to make it, but you always encouraged me to hold on to God! Thank you from the bottom of my heart. I pray God will continue to smile upon you with many more blessings. Love you, sis!

A very special thanks to my friends indeed, Pastors Carl and Sandra Stubbs for ENCOURAGING me to write this book. I thank God for all your love, support and prayers. Most of all, your obedience to God. You are not only my friends, you are family. I pray God continue to richly bless you for all your kindness towards me over the years.

Foreword

"In all thy ways acknowledge Him and He shall direct thy path". Proverbs 3:6

Have you ever listened to someone speak or watched their actions and thought: "What in the world is wrong with them?" Well, I have. Never forming a relationship with that person, you will never really know them. Sometimes, forming our own opinions of a person before we really get to know them, can alter our judgement. Sometimes we view them as mean, rude, insensitive, or judgmental. We may identify them as someone with emotional issues that we just don't have time to deal with. We don't know beneath their hard exterior, are hurting people. I have had the honor of knowing the writer of this book my entire life; and at one point lived in her home. I have not only heard but seen how her issues have affected her in every aspect of her life. Others thought she was a mean and rude person who didn't care. I have seen her silent tears, hurts, and pain that others could not see. I've heard her heart and seen past the exterior walls that others didn't appear to notice. After hearing many times over the years, "hurting people, hurt people", her life is a perfect testament of a person, having not dealt with childhood issues. Being a hurt person for many years, caused her to become emotionally withdrawn and affected many of her relationships. Having to deal with the guilt and shame from all the hurts she caused people, took a toll on her life.

Debrea's story exemplifies how childhood traumas can affect adulthood, when not dealt with. In this book, "A Woman with Childhood Issues", she stops covering up and trying to hide her life issues. She transparently shares key facts, and how those issues have caused her to be totally misunderstood.

While reading this story, please pay close attention to what the writer is saying, and I promise it will change your perspective of other people with a tough exterior; not everything is as it appears. If you truly read it with an open and understanding heart, this book will change your life from this moment on. You may currently have issues of your own that you haven't felt comfortable sharing; however, after reading this book, I pray that it will help you to release your own story. You may be crying for help on the inside; however, displaying a hard, negative, and an insensitive demeanor on the outside, yet being totally misunderstood. The writer now understands that, you will continue to be bound in your mind if you don't become free in your heart.

I encourage you to truly embrace the total raw and uncut story of the experiences that Debrea is now sharing with the world. Today she is on her journey for God; following His will for her life. Sometimes still being misunderstood; however, still trying to do the will of God. Only to be liberated in her life and now able to freely walk in the gifts and calling that God has placed on her life. It will bless your soul and free your mind and heart from your own experiences that have had you bound for years. This story will help you not to judge a book by its cover. Just know, YOU are not alone!

Yolanda Priddy

Issue 1

WHERE MY LIFE BEGINS

The eldest of four children, my mom was born in Yuma, Arizona. My grandmother, for several reasons, left my grandfather and took the children to a small town in Arizona called Gila Bend. My mom was a petite young lady; only about five feet tall and about three pennies over 100 pounds. She was very classy. There couldn't have been too much to do in a town that had few people and even fewer blacks at that time. Everybody knew everybody, so everybody knew everybody's business. My dad was a towering six foot two and 246 pounds. He was a strong handsome young man. My eldest brother looks like my dad as a young man. He was introduced to my mom by his cousin. My dad loved to make you laugh. I would say he was a comedian by nature. He could just say stuff off the top of his head and have you rolling.

My mom said for fun, they would sit on the grass while my dad stood on top of a dirt hill and became the stand-up comedian, making everybody laugh. I think he inherited that from his mom, because she was like that and every one of his siblings could make you laugh at a drop of a hat. My siblings and I inherited that trait. Well, I guess my mom and dad got along well enough for him to capture her attention. My dad asked my mom if he could date her. That sounds so funny coming from your mom, but that's how she told me the story. She said yes; however, he had to ask her mother for permission to take her out on a date to the movies. Back then, going to movie theater was the in thing, I don't believe there was anywhere else to go except the desert.

Gila Bend had lots of cotton fields. While living there my mom became best friends with one of my dad's female cousins. At that time, there were only three black families living there and my mom's family was one of them. My dad and his family moved from Coleman, Texas. They did so because some of his family was already there working in the fields and that's what families did back then. Whenever there was a place that was good for farm work everybody that could – migrated to where the work was. Seems like families worked together more back then. At that time Gila Bend, Arizona was that place.

After dating for two years, my parents decided to take things a little further. They began to see each other every day causing them to become even more emotionally attached. My mom started spending so much time with my dad, her mom decided that they were getting a little bit too close. My mom then decided my grandmother was being a little too strict, so she and my dad planned to run away together.

Somehow, my dad convinced his mom to pick them up and move them both back to Tucson where she lived. One day while my grandmother was out working, my mom and dad packed her things and off to Tucson, they went; without my grandmother's permission. They hadn't lived there long before they decided to move back to Gila Bend, moving in with my grandmother. It was a lot different for them back then, now you would get a good whooping for leaving home without permission. My mom gave birth to six children in this union.

During this transition, my dad lost his father. After the loss of his father, he became very abusive.

He was a heavy drinker and he would beat my mom for no obvious reason. Each time he'd beat her - of course - he would say he was sorry. She believed it because she loved him. It's hard to recognize you're the victim of abuse when you're in love. Well, this abuse lasted for years. One day my dad was beating my mom so bad his mother walked into the room to stop him. Why did he not go to jail? I don't know. From my understanding my grandfather was very abusive to my grandmother. My father saw his father abusing his mother, so I think he thought that is what should be done. To "keep her in line" you just take your fist and beat her.

I don't believe he ever knew all the emotional scars, it left on and in my mom. My mom yet stayed with my dad for many more years. Another time my dad got drunk and asked my mom if she would go down to the café down the street from their house with him. She agreed, but before they arrived there, he took her down to the ravine (a place where they would go fishing) and beat her so badly that he broke her neck. He bashed her head into one of the swings and blackened both her eyes with his fists. She didn't find out her neck was broken until many years later.

A WOMAN WITH CHILDHOOD ISSUES

Based on what my mom could piece together, it seems he would beat her when he had either been with another woman or wanted to be with one. After he beat her this time, he had the nerve to make her go to the café and just sit on a seat in front of everybody. Sitting there like a spectacle and of course not able to say anything because now she's afraid of him. I guess that made him feel like a real man. Well, that to me is not a real man. That was a generational curse in action. Things got better again, with more apologies, my mom stayed. Well, he got drunk again and beat her for the last time. This time my dad fell asleep holding her so she wouldn't get away.

When he fell asleep, she eased out the bed. My dad always carried a pocketknife. He fell asleep with it in his hand. She eased the knife out of his hand. She said she heard this small voice telling her not to throw it on top of the house because that would be the first place, he would look for it so then she decided to throw it in the outhouse. She thought if he goes to get it out of there, he deserved it. He also had a shot gun that she had taken and woven under the springs of the bed. He did wake up looking for his knife. Never finding it. Finally, in 1958 my mom was fed up with all the abuse.

After being with this man and bearing his six children, it was time to leave the situation before she died, and we didn't have a mother or father. My grandmother had a brother that lived in Menlo Park, California. My mom decided that she would go live with her uncle to start a new life. She really wasn't sure what life would be for her when she arrived there so she could not take us with her. She planned her get away. She packed her things when my dad was away, leaving enough things in the closest to make it look as though she was still there.

If he would have had any idea, she was planning to leave him he would have beaten her again and even killed her. Well, she and her two sisters got together and bought her a one-way ticket to California. Things seemed to be going well in California for my mom and my dad didn't hunt her down. My mom left two of her five children (at the time) with her sisters, Ella and Mozella, and me she left me with my aunt Bernice. After several months of settling down in her new life my mom returned to Gila Bend to get us.

At first, my dad was so mad, he decided to keep us after telling my mom she couldn't have us. That didn't last long. I guess the responsibility of so many children scared him, he quickly changed his mind and gave us to our mom. We all went back to California with my mom. Months passed. My mom met and married a new man.

Since most of my mom's family was still in Gila Bend, when Christmas time came, we traveled back for vacation. While there, my mom and stepdad went down to the café to visit people she knew. Somehow, my dad found out she was in town with the kids. He decided he wanted us. My dad went to my grandmother's house to get us. My two older sisters wouldn't go with him unless my cousin who was the same age as them could go. His mom said he could not go and so my sisters chose to stay.

My brother and sister right above me were promised ice cream if they would go with him. I was eighteen months old at the time, so he didn't have to ask me or promise me anything. He simply lifted me from the crib. My mom came back to the house and to her surprise her children had been taken. My mom did try to talk my dad into letting her take us back home with her, but, because he was so angry, he told her no. She called the police and they asked her if he was the father. When she confirmed that he was, they told her he had as much right to have the children as she did. My mom had to go back to California without three of her children.

Months later she came to Tucson, where we were, to get us. Though just a few years old, I remember being pulled by my arms by adults and my dad telling my mom he would not let her have us. He said that would only happen over his dead body. My mom told him that she would not be back to get us and that when we got older, we would come where she was. Eventually, all three of the children were in fact reunited with our mom.

Years passed, and my mom moved to Salem, Oregon. I remember her coming to visit one of my older sisters. At that time, my dad had been living in Oregon for a while and I was living with my sister. My mom knocked on the door, I went to the door to let her in. The look on my mom's face when she saw my dad sitting there, was like seeing breath pulled suddenly from her body. My mom and dad had seen each other many times before, but this time it was different. I could tell my mom was extremely uncomfortable. She had come to see my sister, but she wasn't at home. She stayed and talked to me for a few minutes. As she was on her way out the door, my dad asked if he could talk to her. She had a look of fear on her face and was very hesitant. I didn't blame her. I was glad my mom gave my dad a chance to talk with her.

After being abused all those years she didn't know what to expect. They had never talked about the situation. She let him talk. He asked her to forgive him. He said: "Doe Doe, you were a good wife, I was just stupid. I'm sorry for all the things I did to you. If you would, please forgive me."

That was a beautiful sight for me to see. My mom told my dad: "Yes, I forgive you."

She then left. My dad said to me later: "Your first love is a bugger." He really loved my mom, he just had lots of issues. He really wished things were different and he could go back and change what he had done. He told me he was a fool for what he had done to her.

AS I LOOK BACK

As I look back on what happened to my mom, I can see why I chose the men in my life. I chose men who were abusive. I was choosing my dad. They were not physically abusive but verbally abusive. I also stayed because I thought I loved them, they loved me, and I didn't think anyone else would love me. We tend to choose men that are like our fathers, especially if we didn't get the affirmation from our dads that we should have gotten as young ladies.

I didn't find out until many years later that my mom and dad were never married! I am not sure why she stayed so long or why she kept having children with this abusive man. I told her: "I'm glad you didn't abort me, but I don't think I would have had the second child after he beat me."

She said she really didn't know any better. And, she shared, he wasn't like that when they first met. She had five children by the age of 23 and no education. What was she going to do?

I GET IT

You must know who you are. Nobody will love you if you don't love yourself - first. I still tell myself every day, I am a good woman and I deserve to be loved and treated like a woman. Just because my father was an abusive man doesn't mean I have to be in an abusive relationship.

I have made up my mind that I don't have to accept just anybody or anything from anybody. I have found out who I am in God and who He says I am, and that is who I am.

THERE IS THE SPIRIT

Lord, I pray for all the women that will read my story. Those that feel as though there is no way out. Lord, let them know there is a way out. You are the way. Give them the courage to rise and be all You said they can be. Help them not to just believe in You but to also believe in themselves. If there has been trauma of any kind, I pray that you will heal them in every part of their mind, soul, and spirit. Heal the broken relationships that some have walked away from thinking there's no hope. Wrap your loving arms around them and let them know they too can make it out of any situation with You on their side.

In Jesus Name I pray, Amen.

Issue 2

MY ELEMENTARY YEARS

It baffles my mind and sometimes fills me with sorrow. There are so many things that I just don't remember about my younger years. As we were sitting at my table eating lunch, a cousin and I began to talk about some of the things we did as kids. We reminisced about all the times we would take family vacations. We talked about going to visit our aunt in Galveston, Texas, or cousins in Tulsa, Oklahoma, and of course, we couldn't forget Coleman, Texas. I always liked to go to Galveston because my aunt would take us to the beach and have us show off our dance moves.

    I was a great dancer. I loved to dance, and I didn't have to have a partner. I didn't like slow songs too much; I liked the fast ones. I also didn't like Oklahoma because of the big ticks and mosquitos that would make lunch out of you. When we would go to Coleman, my great-grandfather (papa) had a juju tree that my great-grandmother (big mama) would let us eat fruit from. I loved those jujus. When big mama died, I was too scared to eat anything off that tree because I thought she was looking, and I was going to get a whooping since she wasn't there to give me permission to enjoy. I really enjoyed family time. My cousin and I wondered where did all that go.

I remember, being in the first grade, going to school one day early to play on the rings. One of my school mates and I were playing and having so much fun, we decided to stay past the second bell. When the second bell rang, you knew you were late. When we finally walked into class, our teacher told us not to sit down because she was taking us to the Principal's office. That meant, we were going to get paddled. In those days, it was legal for administrators to spank kids. I remember that day far too well. Mind you, I only got that one paddling and it taught me not to miss that second bell anymore.

Elementary school was fun. I was a Brownie, the younger aged part of the Girl Scouts. When it was time for cookie sales, I would eat all those people's cookies. My aunt didn't know we ate more cookies than we sold. The leftover cookies in the boxes, we would hide in the bushes on our way home from school. Once I was chosen to sell popsicles after school. Those were the days. I couldn't wait for school to be over to go sell those popsicles, even though I ate and stole more than I sold. I would sell to some of the kids, but the ones I called my friends I would tell them to come back when everybody left and just give them one. I took home boxes of popsicles, didn't pay for them, but I took them. I'm sure glad I never got caught stealing that ice cream.

There were five of us young girls that always hung out together, up until the time I moved away. We would have talent shows at school and our group would always volunteer to be one of the preforming groups. Once, during the talent show, we performed as The Supremes. One of the girls in our group could really sing. I don't know how she could sing like that and be so young. She would always be our lead singer. We would have jacks' tournaments (I was incredibly good at playing jacks) and jump rope tournaments. My favorite part of playing jacks was when you had to pick up more than one jack at a time. When you could pick up more than one and not drop any, you just knew you were a skillful player. The boys would always play marbles. I used to love to see them play because the marbles were so pretty in color. It was amazing how hard they could shoot those marbles and they would never break or even crack.

We had a golf course right next to our school, when the players would hit the golf balls, sometimes they would come over the fence onto the school property, the players would then offer us money for each one we would give back. Well, since they were willing to pay for them, we would hop the fence and collect them off their course and then sell them back to them. We didn't call it stealing, we called it making money. Oh, what fun. Glad we didn't get caught. Elementary was fun, wasn't much to do except play.

I loved Christmas and Easter. I think those were my favorite holidays. We would always have a big beautiful silver Christmas tree with all the trimmings. It was so much fun decorating it because I knew there were going to be gifts under it for me. When my aunt would put our presents under the tree, she would often take the light bulb out in the hallway so we couldn't see under the tree. I always wondered how Santa could come down that chimney put the gifts under the tree and never make any noise. For years I believed he was real. When morning would come all these gifts were under that big beautiful tree. Of course, we never saw anyone or heard anyone. Christmas Day would be the day that all the kids would get dressed up and go to the movie theater together. There would always be a special movie playing just for kids. We'd put on our new clothes and off we'd go. You couldn't tell us we weren't cute.

It was during my junior high school years that I discovered I really didn't like school. I think it was because I had more people telling me what to do and you were more accountable than in elementary. I already didn't have a say at home, and at school I was with more people telling me what I can and cannot do instead of asking me sometimes, what do I want to do? I always wondered why I had to learn all the stuff I really didn't think I would be using as I got older, or I really didn't need anyway. I started skipping classes. When I skipped classes I was my own boss.

There was nobody there telling me what I can and cannot do, where I can and cannot go. This was the joy of my life, newfound freedom. I was always a home body; thus, wanting to go to school activities didn't thrill me. My two cousins that I was raised with always wanted me to go to the football games with them. I never liked sports, never saw what anybody got out of watching someone throwing a ball, being tackled when you got it or putting one in a basket. I just wanted to stay home with my mom (aunt). I guess you could say, back then I was a mama's girl to a certain extent.

That day, having lunch with my cousin brought back so much. We laughed about how she used to always pinch me. She said she did it to make her laugh. She would laugh but I thought it was so mean. As a matter of fact, my aunt took us to the studio when we were younger to take a picture together. On this picture, she is smiling, pinching me. I have a frown on my face and of course no one knew why I was frowning. I hated anyone touching my feet, and she knew that. When we would lay in bed, what would she do? She would make sure her feet would touch mine and laugh. That wasn't funny to me because I hated it. I really wasn't into boys back then because we would just chase them and fight them. I guess I should have kept chasing and fighting them, maybe things would have gone a little differently in my life.

With all the things we shared over that meal, it is still strange how there is so much I still cannot recall. It's as though somewhere in my life I stopped existing, dropped off the face of the earth and then reappeared at the age of twelve. Trauma can sometimes take a toll on one's memory, and I believe I am one of its victims.

AS I LOOK BACK

I do remember having some fun times as a child. Too bad childhood doesn't last as long as adulthood. There seemed to be not much to worry about back then. The adults took care of everything for you. I wish now that I'd went to classes in junior high because there is so much in the education part that I missed. I can see now what I missed then. I miss not knowing the rest of how my life went in between those years.

I GET IT

This is what I don't get... why is there a block of memory? Was my childhood so traumatic that it was in my best interest to just block everything? Would I have been able to bear those memories?

What I understand now is that God protects us in several ways. While I may always wonder about those missing parts, I understand that I must trust God with them. Perhaps, as life continues, He will unveil parts. Perhaps, He will keep others hidden. My focus must be on celebrating the testimony that I can live today.

THERE IS THE SPIRIT

God is so amazing. I really believe He has allowed me to block the most devastating part of my life. He protected me all my life, even when it came to remember.

Dear Lord,

Thank you for Your presence during every season and every moment of my life. Thank you for holding those things that you know are too much for me to bear in this season in Your powerful hands. Though I may not remember, though I cannot see – I know that my life has always been securely in Your hands. You have hidden me beneath Your mighty wings, and You continue do so. I trust You with all my mind – even its missing pieces. I submit them all to You.

In Jesus name, Amen.

Issue 3

THEN THERE WAS 12

Life wasn't a piece of cake for me. I never remember having a birthday party or anyone celebrating me in any form for any reason. I always wondered why I was even born. Never knew how I got where I was and why I wasn't with my biological mom. I just remember, her writing me and her letters being thrown to me and my aunt telling me my mom didn't want me. I never believed that. I remember being sad all the time, never really finding that I fit in anywhere. I never knew the purpose for my life. I just wanted to die because I never felt loved. I didn't even know what the word meant, because what I was looking for and what I had experienced surely wasn't love.

At twelve years old, would you expect your life to have so many twists and turns? Do you even know what to expect at that age? How many dreams do you have then? How many tears can you shed? After so much trauma, how do you still manage to survive? GOD!

I never shared any of my secret thoughts with anyone because I never felt safe enough to do so. I had a few friends from my neighborhood who I would go to house parties with, but I never talked to anyone about what was in my heart or on my mind. Most of the time I just talked in my mind because that felt safe and there was no one that would tell what I said to cause me to be beaten for those things. I used to wet the bed. I was so scared when I would wake up and my bed was wet. I would try to hide it, but my aunt would always check. When it was wet, I got beaten. I remember her taking me to the doctor to find out the cause of bed wetting. She told me that if the doctor couldn't find a medical reason, she was going to beat my behind again. I never thought it could be from the trauma I was experiencing. I don't even remember when I stopped. I do remember my days were filled with thoughts of suicide.

I always hated school. I guess because my dad always told me I was going to finish school if that was the last thing, I ever did. He told me he wanted me to be more than just a whore like my older sisters. Imagine being told all your young life that you'll never be nothing but a whore and having a bunch of babies by different men. Wow! What a thing to say to your young child. By the time I turned twelve years old I had decided I had been called a whore and a female dog long enough. I decided that's what I would be. Not knowing the road I was about to take.

My dad would say he loved me, but I really don't think he knew how to love or how to show his kids that he loved us. In hindsight, I learned he wasn't shown love growing up. He would get overly emotional when he was drinking. That's when he would do most of his heart talking. This was the beginning of my rebellious days. With my father's education commands in mind, I enrolled in Tucson High School, never intending to complete it from the beginning. Going to class for me was just to meet whomever I could so I could have someone to skip class with. Most days I just stayed in the parking lot knowing someone would spot me and away we'd go.

Everyone knew if there was someone hanging out in the parking lot, they were ditching class. We liked to go down the street from the school where there were plenty of hippy stores to steal whatever we could get out the stores with. It wasn't far from school and still on the same side of town. Back then we wore a lot of tie-dyed clothes. Those were the days of bell-bottoms and clog shoes. I guess they were called hippy stores because at that time, on the west side of town there were a lot of hippies everywhere. They owned a lot of stores in that area. Hippies worked in the stores and they were always high on weed or whatever, so they never paid attention to what we were doing. I remember, going in the store putting on a pair of elephant leg pants as though I was trying them on. I slid my pants on over them and walked out the store. I was never noticed because there were so many people in the store. Other than the hippie stores, I would hang out downtown in the five and dime stores, stealing. There wasn't a lot of girls that would ditch with me. I was a loner even back then; it was fun at that time because I never got caught.

When I went to class, I never took a book with me. I figured if paper, pencil or a book couldn't fit in my bra then it couldn't go to class. I don't even think I took a purse. By the time I was twelve and in high school I didn't care about my life too much. All I remember was, I wanted to be with my biological mom and nothing else mattered to me. I didn't understand why I couldn't be with her. I never had a choice in the decision that was made. All I knew (before talking with my mom years later) is I was an infant when I was taken, and no one would tell me why.

I was very much interested in "bad boys" at this time in my life. I think I was looking for my dad's love in them. Freddie was the first bad boy I met. After him, that's all I was interested in. Don't know why. For me that was a time that whatever I wanted to do, I did; of course, with consequences. I really didn't care. I didn't care if I lived or died. I just wanted out of the hell hole I lived in. I wanted to live with my mom. All I knew about Freddie was he was a great distraction from my life, and he had two younger brothers; and they all lived with their mom. He was tall and slender. I thought he was attractive. I don't know why he was attracted to me, beyond sex.

I don't know about their father because he never talked about him and I never asked. I knew he came from a broken home and looking back he, himself was just as broken as I was. Freddie was in and out of the boys' home a lot. I don't know the reasons because we never talked about that either. I guess I fell for him because I believed he was nice to me and loved me.

I was looking for love in all the wrong places and there was Freddie. Freddie and I began to start seeing one another. I was sneaking around because my aunt had no idea, I even knew this boy let alone calling myself having a boyfriend. We would meet at school and go wherever we wanted to go all day long. By the time school was out we were back as though we had never left; we just mingled back in with the rest of the students. We would mostly go to someone's house he knew and have sex. I'd catch the bus or walk home from school and he'd go his way. I knew the school would either call my house or send a letter that I wasn't in my classes that day and I knew I would get beaten but I really had lost any sense of caring.

I remember one morning, after being cursed and beaten, I ran into the kitchen and opened the drawer where the knives were. I pulled out the butcher's knife, held it in my hand tightly. I was determined to take my life that morning. I lifted the knife in the air, as I was bringing it down and towards my body - full force, my hand suddenly stopped. Someone pried my fingers apart and I dropped the knife. No one was in the kitchen except me, physically. Someone was there, spiritually. I was so scared I ran to my bedroom and hid. I never shared that with anyone.

Freddy was a dose of relief from all that. For a long time, no one knew we were even seeing each other because no one ever saw us together. Well, as time went on, we got more serious and I started seeing him more and staying out longer with him. I lived on the west side of town and he lived on the south side. One day Freddie called the house for me and my aunt answered the phone. All I heard on my end was a bunch of cursing. I knew Freddie had cursed her because she refused to allow him to talk to me. She told him I was too young to have a boyfriend; of course, she was right. I was twelve and he was eighteen.

He was not going to take no for an answer. By this time, we had been having sex, so now I really didn't see any reason I couldn't see him. Freddie talked to his mom that way all the time so cursing out a lady was normal for him. At that time, I didn't know anything about statutory rape. I was so used to being talked to in a profane and mean manner, I figured it was normal. I also believed that the way he handled her proved he loved me. Someone was sticking up for me; he spoke against my aunt for me. I thought she was being mean and controlling because she wouldn't allow me to see my boyfriend. When their conversation ended, whatever he said to her she took out on me and she got off the phone in a total rage. I was beaten for it and I decided, I was still going to see him. That beating made me even more determined to be with him. He - loved - me.

I remember being beaten so bad that all I wanted was to die. I asked God: "Why don't you just kill me and let me go to hell? Because it must be better than living in this house." That house was hell. Still, I decided I was going to see him against my aunt's wishes. I had run away from home several times and for me that wasn't a problem. I never thought about where I would stay, I just would not go home. I thought that if I kept running away, someone would finally say: "go live with your mom."

I would just hang out at the recreation center where all the youth spent time together. He and I would go to his mom's place sometimes, but not much, I think his mom was afraid of him. One day we met up at school and we went over to one of his friend's house. It was getting late and I knew if I went home, I was going to get the whooping of my life, so we decided to just stay there. One night led to my being gone for three months. After being gone for all those weeks, I heard that the police were looking for me. I was reported as a runaway. They had looked for me everywhere they could, or where they thought I would be. I knew I couldn't go back; I was really going to die.

A WOMAN WITH CHILDHOOD ISSUES

My family didn't even know Freddie. They knew less about him than I did. When we would go places, we would be careful not to go where we thought someone would know us. We were being extremely careful not to be seen, afraid of being picked up by the police. We would see the police, but they didn't see us. He would have gone to jail I'm sure, and I'm sure I might have been beaten to death. By this time, I had been missing for three months. One night we decided to go over on the south side of town to a center where all the young people spent time together. Well, that night we were safe enough to get back to where we were hiding out. We went the next night and the next thing I know my aunt and my cousin showed up. My cousin somehow managed to drag me to the car and force me in it. I remember my aunt reaching in the back seat cursing me and slapping me across the face. I was so terrified because I didn't know what was going to happen to me. She made the next few days more of a living hell than I can recall. I was numb. I didn't care and I think that made her angrier. That became our existence, until…

When we got home, I knew I was in big trouble. First, they had been searching for me for three months. Then they found out I'm not just pregnant, but three months pregnant. I couldn't convince my aunt that I didn't run away to get pregnant. No one ever told me how you get pregnant, so I had no idea I was. I just knew I didn't have any periods all the time I was away, and I was happy about it because I always thought they were nasty. After my aunt found out I was pregnant the real nightmare started. Seriously, NOTHING I had gone through with her could compare to what was to come. She paid close attention to the use of sanitary pads and who was using them. I never gave it a thought. What a crazy and unusual thing to track! It was one sure sign of pregnancy for her. Plus, I was very thin, maybe ninety pounds; but I was all stomach when I came back. Anybody could see I was pregnant.

My grandmother was called into action soon after my in-home pregnancy diagnosis. She and my aunt decided to perform a special ritual on me to end the diagnosis. First, I had to take a tablespoon of castor oil and chase it down with an orange. The command was: "If you spit it out or throw it up, you're going to take some more!" Then, I had to lay in bed for at least one hour while they took an unsharpened pencil and a clothes hanger and stuck them up into my uterus. They were reaching for the unborn fetus to kill it. She would tell me: "You need a baby like you need a hole in your head."

I would lay there in tears, terrified to move, wishing I could just die. I still wonder why they didn't kill me instead of doing that to me. I don't know why my baby had to die and they had all their children. I would say to myself: "if my biological mom was here, she would never do this horrible thing to me or allow this to be done." I even thought, if my dad knew this, he wouldn't allow his mother and his sister to do this to me. I always wanted to be a mom. I wanted to be a schoolteacher at one point in my life. After all that, I had to sit in a hot tub of turpentine water as hot as I could stand it. I had no idea what the purpose of that was. This took place for three months. I couldn't say anything or tell anyone. So afraid they would kill me if I did. I would then get out of the tub and get dressed for school and catch the bus with the rest of the kids.

Back in those days, Tucson High School, had a program where they would help the kids get summer jobs. I had applied for a job and I was hired as an Activity Director working with younger kids in the surrounding area parks. This job would supply lunches for the neighboring children and lots of activities. The park I was assigned to was on the south side of town. Instead of my aunt having to drive me over there every morning before she went to work, she and my aunt, Bernice got together and decided it would be best that I just stayed at her house which made it easier for me to get to work since this park was around the corner from her.

Well, one morning when I arrived at work, and Freddie showed up. We were sitting on one of the benches talking, when a car pulled up and guess who it was. It was my aunt checking on me. She was furious when she saw Freddie talking to me. She fussed and fussed; but allowed me to go back to work and Freddie left. That morning, I had woken up with a bad stomachache. I didn't know what was going on, I just knew my stomach hurt like it had never hurt before. I don't remember the baby ever moving. But again, I didn't know what to expect because I was never taught about getting pregnant, being pregnant or how to know if something was wrong or if it was time for the baby to be born. After her disturbance, those pains returned, powerfully.

The day went on, I finished my shift and went home to my aunt's house. When I arrived, my stomach was hurting so bad I couldn't go to sleep or anything. I still sucked my thumb at this time as my security blanket. This time it didn't work.

My stomach hurt so bad I thought I was going to die. When I arrived at my aunt's house, she wasn't home, but my cousin Doris was there. She told me to lie down on the couch. She asked me if I was pregnant, and I told her, yes. She said: "I suspected it." She didn't want to just come out and ask. She asked me if I wanted something for pain, I told her yes.

She went away and came back with two pain pills. I took them and immediately threw them up because the pain was so great. By this time her mom walked through the door. She told her mom what was happening, and her mom called my other aunt. My aunt and my grandmother arrived in about thirty minutes. They took me into my aunt's bedroom, and by this time the pain was so intense I was getting hot and cold. Well, being that I never had a baby before I did not know I was having contractions. I jumped out of the bed, ran to the bathroom because it felt like I needed to go. That's when my water broke.

While sitting on the toilet, I looked down and I saw this tiny baby (fetus) curled up in the toilet with little hands, eyes, feet and ears. It was dead. It just looked as if it was a big blood clot. There were all these cords still connected to me. Not knowing what was going on and not really knowing what to do, I got a piece of toilet paper and began to pull everything out. I then flushed the toilet. My aunt came into the bathroom and I told her what I had done. She said: "thank God!"

She had been praying that I would abort that baby. By the time the baby was aborted I was thirteen. We went back home to my aunt's house where I grew up. I never told Freddie what happened to the baby. He got locked up again and we never saw each other again. Days passed and my stomach started hurting bad again. My aunt accused me of sleeping with another boy. I didn't want to see another boy after what I experienced. Weeks passed and I began to hemorrhage. I couldn't get out of the bed. I had to sleep with a big black garbage bag on my bed and two Kotex sanitary napkins on because I was passing huge blood clots. One night one of my cousins came over, she told my aunt she needed to take me to the hospital before I bled to death.

The next day my aunt made an appointment for me to go to the doctor. She told me before we got there that if I told the doctor what she had done to me, she would kill me. Being thirteen and physically and verbally abused all the time, I wasn't going to tell. I feared for my life. We got to the doctor's office and she insisted on going to the examination room with me; however, they wouldn't let her. The doctor examined me then he asked me had I ever been pregnant. My answer was an immediate no.

He gave me two little white pills. I took them and the hemorrhaging stopped. I never got pregnant after that, but I still was physically and verbally abused for whatever I did. At this point, my aunt didn't know I had dropped out of school. I was going along with the routine. I would leave home like I was going to school, but that's not where I ended up most of the time. I met this young man - Mac. He was dark, handsome, and bowlegged, and he attended the high school I was enrolled in. Mac wasn't a bad boy at all. He was well liked and a senior at Tucson High. Unlike me, he attended classes like he was supposed to. We only saw each other at school or house parties. Mac and I had more of a sexual relationship than a committed one. I never ran away again because Mac wasn't that kind of guy. He only ditched with me once, and it was clear he wasn't comfortable with that. I liked Mac a lot, there was something different about him that certainly had my attention, and his family was genuinely nice. I went to school to spend time with Mac. The rest of the time I did whatever I pleased and that was driving my aunt out of her mind.

My aunt finally got tired and decided that I should go live with my dad. I transferred schools and I grew more rebellious because I really didn't want to go live with him. I remember my dad telling me that my uncle and aunt wanted to adopt me. I cried and said no, he asked me why, I never told him. I couldn't tell my dad that if he gave me to his sister, she would kill me, and it would be legal – or so I thought. I was thirteen and what I knew better than anything else was being cursed and beaten. Living with my dad was no better.

My dad already had one of my other sisters, my older brother, and a girlfriend that had three children of her own that he wasn't taking care of. His girlfriend was the one that told my aunt that if I came to live with them, she would leave my dad. I did not want to be the cause of her leaving him even though he beat her all the time. I was afraid of my dad. He beat my brother once until his nose bled. He beat my sister when she was holding her infant child in her arms. That was not the place I wanted to live. I just knew it was a matter of time that he would kill one of us.

One Friday night my dad's girlfriend's daughter asked my dad if I could go to a party with her. It took him a long time to answer. He called me in his room and hesitantly said yes. He then told me to be home by twelve. I said okay. We left the house headed for the party. We went, she came home at the time she was supposed to. Well - me - I said to myself: "he said twelve, but he didn't say which day." I went home at noon the next day. I'll never forget, my dad was watering the front lawn. He saw the car drive up and the young man that brought me home. He laid the hose down; went into the house and I already knew I was going to get beaten.

Well, I went into the house. He beat me and I didn't cry. I had no more tears. All those years of being beaten and crying for my mom, and by his family, I was cried out. I remember saying to myself one day I'm not going to cry anymore. One day, they will be crying over me. I would sit and think of my funeral and see people crying for me, pouring out all the tears I had cried. When my dad saw that I wasn't crying, he threw the belt down and said the next time he whooped me, he would be whooping me with his fists. I lived with them a brief time longer. My dad didn't know that I had contacted my mom. I always had her address. My sister, Vera always stayed connected with me. She gave me my mom's phone number and I called her. I had been talking to her for several months making plans to run away to live with her.

I made plans without announcing to anyone that I was going to go live with my mom. My mom had moved to Oregon at this time. They were on vacation in Gila Bend, Arizona visiting my mom's family. I asked my mom would she get me so I could go back and live with her. She had no idea what had been going on in Tucson. Because she was visiting Arizona already, getting me from Tucson would be easier. This meant I was finally leaving. There was one person I needed to tell and that was Mac.

When mom arrived, Mac had come to visit me that day and we were out taking a walk. I told him I was moving to Oregon, but we would keep in touch. Turns out, Mac's family was moving to Nevada. We were going to have say goodbye anyway. Mac went on his way; and I went on mine – finally with my mom. I know if my dad had been home that day, I would have never been able to leave. It would have been bad! I never told my mom that my dad didn't know I was leaving nor that he didn't want me to. I did hear after I left, he beat his girlfriend for allowing me to leave.

AS I LOOK BACK

I'm glad that I didn't have a child at thirteen. I'm not glad it was taken. I don't know at this point how many babies I would have had without a father to help raise them. You know, because the father was always in trouble, would I have had to deal with the same trouble his mother dealt with? I was a broken and abused child when that baby was conceived. It was conceived in a place of false love, false concern and desperation. I would have loved it the best I knew how, but the best – then – was distorted at best.

I GET IT

I don't get why my child was taken the way it was taken. That is still something I think of today. I think I would have rather given it birth and had the child raised by someone who could love it. To have it brutally assaulted in my womb is a pain that I still bear. To be so disconnected from what was growing inside of me that I could simply flush it away shows the depth of darkness that trauma and abuse can drag you into. What I do know is that even in the harshest of times, we can heal physically, and we can heal spiritually – if we want to.

THERE IS THE SPIRIT

Dear Father,

My strength, my Lord and my Redeemer. All I can say is: "God You know what's best." You have been with me all the time. I know that now. God thank you for choosing me to go through this. Thank you for giving me the strength, through heavy tears, doubt and reservations, to be able to share my hurt and healing with someone else.

God, I rest in THIS PURPOSE that You have in me. To speak life into every woman that has been where I have in her own way. I honor the assignment and I agree with my anointing to fulfill it.

In Jesus name, Amen!

Issue 4

MY JOURNEY TO OREGON

I was sixteen years old and, on my way, to live in Lebanon, Oregon with my mom, stepdad and five of my siblings, who I really didn't know. I met them all when I went to visit at the age of twelve. My mom had been vacationing in Oakland, California with her brother and his family. We stopped by to pick up my siblings. It was nice to get a chance to finally meet my uncle and his family; but we didn't stay there long. Up early and away we went, on the way to my new home. When I finally arrived in Lebanon, a place I had never been before, it was very cold. I thought it would never stop raining. It rained for the three months; non-stop! There were only four black families that lived in this town and two of them were relatives. Those being my mom's and my eldest sister's. I had a sister that lived in

Salem; so, I went there one weekend to spend a few days with her and her family.

It was great because she didn't have to work, and we spent a lot of time together getting to know each other. This sister would come to Tucson a lot to visit us, so I knew her a little more than I did my other siblings there. One day, my eldest sister and her family came to visit us in Salem. When they drove up, there was this "fine" young man sitting in the back seat of the car. Of course, I had to be a little nosey and see who it was. I played it off though like I was really interested in talking to my sister and brother-in-law. I didn't want this man to think I was running to the car to see him even though I was. My brother-in-law introduced us.

I guess my brother-in-law and sister knew we were interested in each other, so my sister asked if I wanted to go back to Lebanon with them. I jumped at that opportunity. This man was tall, dark and a whole lot of handsome. I got some clothes from my sister's house and got in the car. Away we went. We talked all the way back. By the time we got to Lebanon, which was less than thirty minutes, me and this gentleman had become really acquainted. I spent a lot of time at my eldest sister's house. I had dropped out of school and had no plans or desire to go back to any school. My sister and her husband did the things I liked to do. They got high. My mom was an Evangelist and I knew I couldn't do that stuff at her house and I wouldn't have wanted to anyway. I was so grateful to be with her after everything that had happened. And I really did (and do) believe in respecting my parents.

The man I met was a good friend of my brother-in-law and I knew he would be coming over every day. Well, my sister and brother-in-law loved smoking weed. I had smoked weed a long time ago, in Arizona. I would only allow my cousin's boyfriend to get weed for me because I trusted he wouldn't give me anything that would harm me. My brother-in-law worked at the only sawmill in town. Every day I would go over to my sister's house, and we would get high. That was the life! I thought, nothing could be better than this. My gentleman friend, Sam would come over to smoke weed as well. Things progressed with us. Remember; before I left Arizona, I was still seeing my high school sweetheart, we had planned to someday see each other again and be together.

I hadn't told Sam about Mac at this time because we had become sexually involved. We met in September of 1973, he proposed to me and we got married in December of that same year. I know, fast, huh? I turned seventeen in November, he asked my mom to sign for me, she knew that was what I thought I wanted, so she did, and we got married. A few weeks before we said I do, I got up enough nerves to write Mac to let him know I was getting married. Well, he didn't take it well. He sent me a letter, only I could read, and his words – well – clearly showed what he thought about the marriage and what he thought about me. We ended on that note; and I never spoke to him again, until years later.

Sam was living in a one-bedroom apartment. He gave up his apartment and we moved into the house with my sister and her family. We lived with them for quite some time; and that was good because that's where I learned to cook. My brother-in-law was an excellent cook.

After we found an apartment down the street from where he worked, we then moved into our own place. When I married Sam, he didn't know I was having an affair with a married man that lived in the same town. I'd met this man before Sam; actually, during earlier visits to Oregon. We were attracted to each other and that was about it, then. When Sam would go to work this man would come to the house. He knew what Sam's work schedule was because they worked together. One day, Sam got up to go to work as usual and I played the role - as always - like everything was alright. Sam would always come home for lunch because we lived down the street. This day my gentleman friend came over during the lunch hour. We were in the bedroom. I heard a knock on the door and then I heard someone pulling at the screen. I knew it was Sam because we never locked the screen only the door. He knew something was up because that day the screen was locked. Well, when I went to the door to let him in; my friend ran out the door with his shoes in his hands. I was caught. How in the world was I going to explain this?

We talked about what had happened and he took me over to the man's house so that I could tell his wife what happened. Of course, I went, in tears but I went. We went over to his house and when he saw us his eyes got big! He didn't know why we were there and what was about to happen. We walked into the house. I asked his wife if I could speak to her. I remember this like it was yesterday. She was in the kitchen cooking. She said yes and came out and sat down at the dining room table. I began to tell her what happened that day. She looked at me, told me she forgave me and then said: "someday, this will happen to you. Some woman is going to do you the same way." We left and went home.

That relationship didn't stop. You know when you're full of lust you think that you must have what you must have, and you really don't consider who gets hurt. I really didn't realize how hurt Sam was and the damage I did not only to the man, but to his family and mine. During the time we lived in Lebanon, I had been trying to have children. I always wanted children. I had not told Sam that there was a possibility I couldn't have children because I didn't know myself. Each month I would pray and hope I was pregnant. Each month I had my cycle and there was no baby.

One day we decided to get checked out. I knew it wasn't him because he had a daughter by a previous relationship in Ohio. I suspected it was me, but I really didn't know and was hoping it wasn't. Well, we went. The doctor said he was able to have children. When they checked me, I had some serious challenges. The botched abortion had done more physical damage than I could have known. I had so much scar tissue that the doctor said it was a 50-40 chance that I could get pregnant. We opted for a surgical procedure to increase those chances. I was scared because I didn't know what was going to happen. I still didn't come clean about the abortion, with Sam. To tell you the truth, I never thought I would have to talk about that wicked and painful procedure. It was something I only talked about in my mind. I was already feeling I wasn't a real woman; how could I tell the man that really loved me, I can't have his child because a homemade abortion was performed on me.

After hours of surgery, I felt like I was hit by a truck. The doctor came in and explained what he had done. He said, the scar tissue was far more prevalent than originally thought. The procedure took longer that he expected. He told me my uterus was behind my ovaries and everything had been matted together because I had been bleeding internally. I thank God I didn't die. I knew I had very painful periods, but I never thought that was the cause. How could I know that I was bleeding internally, and my reproductive organs were locked up in matted tissues? I cried for weeks. I finally had to tell my husband the horrible story of what happened to me. We sat and cried together. At that time my older brother and my husband had become particularly good friends. My brother came over and I had to tell him the story he never knew. I healed from the surgery and I kept praying each month that I would have a baby. Sam's job ended and we moved to Salem to get a fresh start with our marriage.

I started going to church with my mom. One Sunday, I decided to give having a relationship with the Lord a chance. I came home a new woman. Life was great. Before I got saved, Sam was very controlling. He was 26 and I was 17. I married him because I thought I would be grown, could do my own thing and nobody would ever run my life again. I knew nothing about life. I went from my aunt's house to my dad's, then from my mom's to Sam's. He was so much more mature than I was. I married a man I didn't love. I was still in love with my sweetheart Mac. I wanted a baby so bad; I prayed all the time for one. I remember telling God if someone placed a baby on my doorstep, I wouldn't even report it. It didn't have to be a black baby either. I just wanted a baby no matter what.

I remember being awakened from a dream hearing the Lord calling my name. It was so clear, it seemed as though it was coming out of the walls. He said: "Debbie, you're going to have a baby." I was so excited. I woke Sam out of a deep sleep to let him know the good news; however, because he didn't hear it, he didn't believe it, even until the day we divorced. I kept attending church, kept hoping every month that I would conceive. I didn't.

A WOMAN WITH CHILDHOOD ISSUES

I left God and got into a new affair. One night I hooked up with the new man at a restaurant. My husband came in this place with a newspaper under his arm. I knew Sam had something rolled up in that paper. We were sitting at the table, Sam walked in and said to me: "move away from the table." I refused to move because I knew if I did, he would shoot this man. You see how the devil will make you bold? Now, if he had shot me, I would have been dead over someone else's husband. Sam left and we got out of that place. We kept seeing each other (the man and I). I guess you could say the devil had hold of me.

I had given my life to the Lord months before, but I wanted this man, so I left God and finally left my husband to be with this man. It wasn't a good thing. The Lord then gave my lover and his wife a mind to move to California. It was over. I lost my husband over someone that was never going to be mine in the first place. I did learn something to pass on. Leave married men alone. You will never win. If they ever leave their wives for you, then you will be the one blamed. It will never work because you were never meant to be together. I moved on, got an apartment, and a year later Sam and I ended up in divorce court.

AS I LOOK BACK

I really believe Sam did love me. I regret all the things I put him through. I know he had many scars added to his life by me. There is never a reason to go outside of your marriage for anything and there is never a good reason to leave the Lord. I often wonder what would have happened if Sam and I would have stayed married. I know that God works all things out for our good, but I still wonder - sometimes.

I GET IT

If there is anything that I can pass on to any woman, it is this: love the one that loves you. My grandmother always said: "a man sees his wife even before she sees him". Women can grow to love men, but men never grow to love women.

THERE IS THE SPIRIT

I have so much to Thank God for. The situations with the adulterous relationships could have gone in horrible directions. I really could have lost my life. But, in the spirit, there was someone praying for me, likely my mother and others in the church where I accepted salvation.

I thank God for the prayers that went up for me. There were cries of mercy for me at this time of my life. I was searching for love "in all the wrong places" and they knew, and God knew that the real love I needed was in Him and in Him alone.

Issue 5

MY LIFE GETS MORE INTERESTING

I moved into my own apartment. I was so sad and lonely. I had been married to my first husband for thirteen years. I must admit, he wanted to get back together before the divorce was final, but I didn't want him back. I was finally free from a man I never loved in the beginning.

While living the single life, I was yet still married. Oh, I filed the divorce papers in that 12th year, but kept them for one year before I allowed the judge to finally sign them.

Months passed. Out of nowhere, I woke up one morning with my old sweetheart Mac on my mind. I should have known it was a trick from the devil. Then, I thought I was the cat's meow and I dared a dog to bark. Mac had given me his sister's phone number. Before I called her, I called every person in Henderson, Nevada with his last name. There were only three families with that last name, so it made it quite easy. I called a number that ended up being his parents' home. His mother and I spoke for a brief time. She did remember meeting me in Arizona. She told me he was living with his sister in another state, and gave me the phone number, so I called it. When I spoke to his sister, she informed me that he wasn't there.

We talked for quite some time and she made a statement that should have made me forget talking to that man all together. She said: "He's my brother but I wouldn't recommend him to my cat." I should have hung the phone up, tore up the number and asked her not to even let him know I called. But no, I left a message for him to call me along with my phone number. Early the next morning, my phone rang. To be honest with you I had forgotten I tried to contact him. I was wondering who was calling me that time of morning?

I picked up the phone and this smooth voice on the other end asked: "Debbie?"

I said: "Yes."

He asked again: "Debbie Jackson?"

I said: "yes" again. He said: "Baby, this is Mac". I slid off my couch like butter onto the floor. I hadn't talked to this man in thirteen years. I don't even know what I was thinking. I guess my little mind went back all those years thinking things would be the same. I started out like I had just talked to him yesterday. Well, we talked so much and so long every day that my phone got turned off because the bill was so high, I couldn't pay it and he never offered. I had so many clues now that I look back. Still, looking for love in all the wrong places.

About three months passed and we made plans for him to come to Salem, Oregon to live with me. Yes, I was still married but I knew I was divorcing Sam. Wow! What a happy day. I was finally going to be with the man that I've always wanted to be with. Finally, it was going to happen. I was in la-la land. The day finally came for Mac to arrive at the bus station and I was right there to pick him up. I was dressed to the hilt. I put on my best dress and was smelling good! He stepped off that bus and I thought I had died and gone to heaven.

He looked the same, still black, bow-legged and fine. I gave him the biggest hug. We laughed and we went home. I had lost my mind, a man I hadn't seen in thirteen years. What was I thinking?

Well, he came on in and everything was perfect. I wasn't working at that time because I had a back injury from my job. He got a job and had no problem working. I thought, this is good. He did drink and smoked his weed. I thought that was okay because he did what he did at the house. He didn't really go out to the clubs.

Now, let me say something right here. Just because they stay at home and do what they do, that doesn't mean they're not doing something! We had this Caucasian girl for a neighbor. She had a little girl that was bi-racial. The lady didn't really visit me, so I didn't think anything about it. Now, remember I had left the church. I started going back to church and felt very guilty because I knew this man should not have been living with me because we were not married. But I couldn't marry him because I was still legally married to Sam.

On Mac's birthday, my neighbor and her little girl came over to the house. I was standing in the kitchen when her little girl went into our bedroom, saw Mac on the bed and said: "hi daddy". You know sometimes we know what we try to ignore. Well, I didn't say anything, but I wondered why that little girl was calling my man daddy. My neighbor said she wanted to make my man a birthday cake. I said: "no, thank you." I told her I would make him one. I was really trying to be nice and not go off. Now, why was she so comfortable asking to make my man a cake for his birthday? I'm thinking, this man has not been here long enough for nothing to be going on; and; of course, I know I'm satisfying him in the bedroom.

Well, remember, I started attending church again. I went to sleep one night and had a dream that Mac was going out of our back door into her back door. It was so real when I woke up, I confronted him. He denied it and me, with my crazy self - believed it. On major holidays, all the family would get together and go to the park for a picnic. One fourth of July we went to the park. I had to go early because I was one of the people who would barbeque. As I was cooking, my baby sister came over to the grill where I was and said: "Debbie, I wish I could tell you something." My sister would always use codes when she really wanted you to know something and she didn't want to come out and just say it. She knew if she just came right out and told me, I wouldn't take it well and I was going to leave that park and go to fight. Well, I asked her what it was. She tried not to tell me, so I questioned her a little more. I asked her: "was it about Mac?". She said: "yes." I asked: "was it about another woman?" She said: "yes." I asked: "was she black or white?" She said: "white." I knew!

I had been babysitting this lady's two young children. She had been asking for their toothbrushes. The lady was at the park and I thought, this is the perfect time to go back to the house to get them. I knew if I acted a fool my sister was not going to allow me to leave that park, so I had to keep my cool. Oh, how hard that was. I stood there and cooked for a few minutes longer, but I had a getaway plan. I needed to get those toothbrushes for these kids to give to their mother. Finally, after I thought it was safe to leave, I went to the lady and told her I was going to my house to get the kids' toothbrushes. I asked my sister to take over cooking until I get back. I gave her the fork and off I went.

On the way there, I decided this was the perfect time to jump on the woman and beat her down for messing with my man. As I pulled up to the apartment the devil said to me: "remember Mac has a 357 magnum up under the bed. Why don't you just put one bullet in the woman, one in the baby and put one in him?" Now, see how the devil works? The baby had nothing to do with this. After the devil said that, the Lord said: "he's telling you what to do, but he's not telling you the consequences." Our doors were right next to each other. I went into my apartment got the toothbrushes and when I came out the door, I went right next door and knocked. No answer. I knocked several times with no answer. Well, I decided to go ahead and leave. As I was starting the car, I looked back at the apartment window and saw her little girl pull the curtains back looking out the window, I knew she was at home. I climbed back out of my car and went back to her door. As I stood there, the devil said: "when she opens that door hit her right in the mouth." This was a woman with a very smart mouth. As I was standing there my whole spirit calmed down. I knew someone was praying for me. She opened the door.

I asked: "Dawn, can I come in?"

She responded:" Right now?"

I insisted "Yes!". She was a person that stayed up late and slept in late. She let me in, when I got in the living room, I heard the Lord say: "walk over to the window and put your hands behind your back." I did.

I said to her: "Dawn, I'm going to ask you a question and please don't lie to me for my sake." She simply said: "okay." Then I asked her the question: "Dawn, have you been sleeping with Mac?"

She hesitated for a few minutes and then began to cry. I already knew the answer. My mind went back to the lady who told me years earlier, that this would happen to me. Dawn looked at me and said: "Debbie, please don't hate me." She said: "every time you would go to church, he would come out of your back door into mine."

That was the dream the Lord showed me. I looked at her. I couldn't even be mad. I just looked at her, smiled and said to her: "I'm not mad at you, I feel sorry for you because you remind me of me some years ago." She cried, and she cried. I said to her: "Mac is coming home as soon as he sees I'm not coming back to the park. When he comes, I'm going to get you for you to come over. I will be asking you the same question in front of him and please don't lie for my sake."

She begged me not to make her come over when he comes because she said, he's going to be mad, hit her and start calling her a whore. I told her if he hits her, I will be pressing charges and I will send him to jail. I said, he is the biggest whore going. Now, I was numb, I didn't know what to say. She asked me for a hug. I gave her a big hug and went out the front door. There was a neighborhood park down the street. I walked down the street to that park, sat on the curb, looked up to heaven and said: "I know this is a dream, this woman did not just tell me she slept with my Mac." This was unreal. I started pinching myself. After a while I went back to my apartment. I knew Mac would soon be coming home because it was getting late and I hadn't gone back to the park after leaving to get the toothbrushes. I went and laid in my bed. Still numb, I could not believe what was happening.

I heard a car come up on the gravel. I thought, "there he is." It was my little sister; she was ducking all the way to the door. When I opened the door, I asked her why she was ducking. She said: "Mac got that gun in there and I didn't want you to shoot me."

I told her I'd never do that. She begged me not to shoot him. I simply asked her to leave. After she left, my other sister pulled up with her sister-in-law. I opened the door, and they came in begging me to give Mac another chance. Shortly after they left, Mac finally came home. When he came in, I went out the door. He knew where I was going. I went next door, brought Dawn over and asked her the same question in front of him. She was crying. He was furious. It didn't matter; the cat was out the bag.

After she left, I told him to pack his clothes and get out of my house. I told him to put my key on the table and get out. He started packing his things and he was on the bus the next morning on his way back to Henderson, Nevada. Now, before the man got to Nevada, I was calling him telling him to come back. The next morning, the Lord woke me up early and gave me a scripture, **2 Corinthians 6:14: "DO NOT BE YOKED TOGETHER WITH UNBELIEVERS. FOR WHAT DO RIGHTEOUSNESS AND WICKEDNESS HAVE IN COMMON? OR WHAT FELLOWSHIP CAN LIGHT HAVE WITH DARKNESS?"**

It couldn't have been any plainer than that. I was on my knees praying. I was telling God how much I wanted THAT man. I told the Creator, the Man who made the man: "I want him! - I want him and you don't know him like I do!" Can you believe that? I said this to God!

He said to me: "I'm going to let you have him, but I'm going to let you see what you're going to get."

I didn't think I would get anything bad. I was happy He said I could have him. I totally misunderstood what He said – TOTALLY! Mac came back within three days. We decided to get married. We went to the courthouse because I already knew I was wrong, and I knew what the Lord had said. I couldn't go to my Pastor for counseling because I knew he was not going to agree and would not marry us; and I really wanted that man. We made an appointment for a Justice of the Peace and got married. I blamed my two witnesses for a long time for signing the papers. The judge signed the divorce papers because (like I said before) I had held them for an entire year, meaning we lived together for one year before we married. I divorced and got remarried right away.

On the way home this man changed to a man I knew I should not have married. I mean that same day on the way home he changed. The Lord opened my eyes to what He had spoken to me. This man started going out to the clubs (without me). This man started seeing all types of women. Early one morning I heard a car pull up on the gravel. The car door opened, and the dome light came on. This man (my husband) was in the back seat hugged up with a woman. I was lying in the bed with tears running down my face. I never let him see me cry.

He would go to church with me every now and then. I decided I was going to go without him. I needed something to hold on to while misery found its way back into my life. Even though he would go, sometimes, he still lived a whole life without me.

I still wanted children. I was still seeing a fertility doctor. One day the doctor called and asked if I was still interested in a child? I told him yes. I was so excited. He said there was a young lady who was planning to give her baby up for adoption and he wondered if my husband and I would be interested? I told him, I would talk with my husband and get back to him. I talked to Mac and he agreed to go and meet with the attorney of the young lady who was pregnant to see what this was all about. We made an appointment to go all the way to Portland to meet with this attorney. When we got there, to my surprise, the young lady that was pregnant was a young lady I already knew. I had no idea she was pregnant. We talked with them and the attorney informed us that she and the young lady would have to talk this over and get back to us.

At this point my husband asked her, how much this was going to cost us. Well, she told us fifteen thousand dollars. Now, mind you we did not have this kind of money, we had to borrow the gas money from Salem to Portland to get to the appointment. Mac looked at the attorney and said: "we don't have that kind of money." I stepped in and said: "my father has the money." The attorney looked at me and inquired if that was true. I said:

"yes." She had no idea I was talking about my "Heavenly Father". The attorney told us the young lady would be the one to decide but they would have to talk about it. Right then, the young lady spoke up and said: "I want them for my baby's parents." I was so shocked and so happy.

I could tell the attorney wasn't happy with her statement. She tried to get the young lady to wait a few days, but she said, "I want them to raise my baby." She said: "I know she goes to church and I want my baby to be raised in the church."

We all shook hands and Mac and I drove back to Salem. On the way back he expressed his disapproval with paying that kind of money and besides we didn't have it. We went to see them on a Friday. That Saturday morning in the shower, the Lord said: "You know the birth mom; call her, make an agreement. Cut out the attorney and make an agreement between you all." I went through a few phone numbers to get her mother's number because I knew she lived with her mother. After getting the number, I called and told her who I was and what I wanted. I asked if I could speak to the young lady and she put her on the phone.

I asked her how much she was getting paid for giving her baby to that adoption agency. She said nothing. I asked her how many dogs cost that much money. We laughed. I then told her what the Lord had said to me that morning. We agreed to knock out the attorney and do this ourselves. We had planned for Mac and me to be at the hospital when she delivered and just take the baby. Well, we didn't know that was illegal. I called an attorney's office and got information on how to do this legally. He gave me the information and I hired him. In the end, it cost five hundred dollars for all the paperwork.

When the baby was born, we were called to the hospital to see him. She had asked me previously for a name for a baby boy. I gave her the name and she named him what I had chosen. I had wanted a baby and testified what the Lord had promised me for so long. I was given three baby showers. The day came for us to get the baby. We got him and our life was complete, I thought.

I had started working for the newspaper and I had to be at work at midnight. I had gone to lay down about seven o'clock so I could be ready to go to work that night. Little did I know, Mac had gotten hooked on crack cocaine. As I lay there in my bedroom trying to sleep, I heard my baby crying. He was crying an unusual cry. I laid there as long as I could. When I got up, I went into the living room to find Mac's legs around my baby's neck in a scissor position. I screamed for him to get his legs from around my baby's neck. My child was screaming. Mac finally got up off the floor. He pushed me. It scared me; but I pushed him back. I went into the kitchen, opened my drawer looking for my knife. Every woman knows where her knife is.

I had gone through so much with this man, I was ready to be done with the whole relationship. When I walked into the kitchen, Mac was right behind me. He spun me around, pushed me up against the counter, pulled his blade out of his pocket and asked: "is this what you're looking for?" He then threw me on the floor, straddling my body with his. He placed his knees on my elbows, took his left thumb and placed it over my windpipe and in his right hand he held his blade on my throat. My baby was standing just a few feet from us looking at all this, screaming. I was begging for my life.

He looked me dead in my eyes and said: "I am the devil, and I'm going to kill you!"

At this point my whole life flashed before me. I just knew I was dead on my way to hell. Remember, the Lord said: "I'm going to let you have him, but I'm going to let you see what you're going to get." All those things played back to me. I begged Mac to let me up to go outside to get some air. After, what seemed like hours, he finally let me up. He then said to me: "I'm going to show you what it's like to have a barrel looking down your face." Years earlier, I had pulled his .357-magnum on him.

As he was walking down the hall, I knew I had to get out of that house. I couldn't take my baby, but I knew he wouldn't hurt him, the devil was trying to kill me. As I walked out the door, I first went over to the right where there were no neighbors, then I turned to the left and headed to the neighbor's house. I heard Mac calling my name, but I just kept walking. He had pressed on my windpipe so hard I could barely breathe or talk when I reached the door of my neighbor. I didn't even knock, I just opened their door and walked in. I told them some of what had happened and asked if they would call the police. They did.

The police took us both to jail because it was domestic. My niece got my son. I was in jail for about an hour and my brother came to get me. I went to my niece's house and never went back to live with Mac. He said, he was not trying to kill me, he was just trying to scare me. I told him he had done an excellent job. One day when I knew he was at work, I went and collected me, and my baby's clothes and I never went back. We lived with my niece until I got back on my feet. I then moved into another apartment with just my son. Mac lived in that apartment with another woman until we divorced, and he moved back to Henderson with his family until he passed away.

AS I LOOK BACK

I see why the Lord said not to marry this man. I don't regret having my son, but I paid a price for marrying someone that I hadn't seen in thirteen years. You really don't know a person anymore after all that time. And when I look back at things, Mac and I really didn't have a relationship back in high school. I think I was in love with being in love.

I also learned through this experience that it is important to listen to what the Lord tells you. To seriously listen to Him and inquire about His words to you and what He may be trying to spare you from. Loving a man can feel like a lot of things; but we must always ask ourselves if that love is anywhere near what God offers.

I GET IT

Sometimes, you just need to leave well enough alone. It is better to be alone than to take yourself or your children through a lot of drama. Pay attention to the things that don't seem right. The red flags are waving for a reason. God is revealing things that are the truth and that's what we need to see it as. The truth can look like a lie when we hear based on how we want our bodies to feel. Like I said, it is better to be alone than to take yourself through a lot of drama. God has promises – not drama – for you.

THERE IS THE SPIRIT

When God says "no" He means no. It was a clear "no" for me, but of course like most of us women, we think we can change that man. Who God has for you is for you and no one else. Lesson learned.

Dear God,

For every woman who has read this chapter and has faced the very face of the enemy in someone she believes loves her and someone she has even asked you to allow in her life; I ask that Your grace and mercy cover her. God, I ask that Your compassion surround her. I ask that You open a way of escape for her and her children. God, I pray that she will get to safety and that she will rest in Your arms so that her heart, her spirit and her body can heal.

In Jesus name, Amen!

Issue 6

ONE MORE CHANCE (LAKE OF FIRE)

I had been separated from my then husband of eight years about six or seven months. My life consisted of going to church, work and taking care of our four-year-old son. I was a single mom living the single life. I did not have any plans to get involved in another relationship. Of course, I'm separated so that should have been a safeguard against that anyway. Being single again for me was good. I decided I would just raise my son and live the single life in God.

Many months down the road I received a phone call from one of the ministers of the church I was attending, who I'd known for many years. I didn't think it was a big deal because as far as I was concerned, I was not interested. I was saved and safe. Family members were telling me he had been interested in me for a long time, but I didn't give that man the time of day nor did I think of him on my list of men for me. The Bible says in Matthew 26:41 "Watch and pray, so that you will not fall into temptation, the spirit is willing, but the flesh is weak."

He would call me every day and we would have engaging conversations. I would talk to him about my failed marriage. I wasn't sad about it. I knew it was over and I had become okay with it. It was nice to have someone to talk to as a friend. We laughed and talked for months. He was a great listener and he never condemned me or said anything bad about my soon to be ex-husband, he just allowed me to vent.

One evening he called and as I began to share, he stopped me right in the middle of it and asked me a question that really caught me off guard. He asked me if I had ever thought how it would be to be married to him? I was speechless. That was very odd for me being a woman that can talk when I need too. I waited for a few seconds and then I asked him a question.

"What did I do for you to ask me that? Did I flirt with you, not knowing that I was doing it?"

He chuckled and said: "no." He explained that he had been interested in me for a long time. Well, what does a woman say after that statement. I was nervous because I didn't know where things were going to go from there; however, I did answer his question and the answer was no, I never gave it a thought because I never looked at him in that way. We continued talking every day. No big deal, just friends. He had two children of his own, I knew them well.

One day I decided to give this man a chance. I thought it would not hurt anything to see what he's about. So, we began to date. We both knew I was still married. He called one day and told me he asked Mac if it was over with us because he wanted to marry me. I thought: "who does that?" I was surprisingly a little hurt when he told me Mac said he was done. Deep down I knew, and I also knew I would never be going back to him anyway. We continued to see each other, and things got serious.

It was a normal day like any other day. I woke up that morning got ready for work in the same manner as usual. Off to work I went dropping my son off to the babysitter. Thinking all day about being with the man I was soon to marry. That day turned out to be the most important day of my life, although very unusual. I had no idea what was in store for me. As my day at work ended, I had planned a date night with my fiancé. He and his children were coming over that evening to watch movies with my son and me. This was not unusual; we did this quite often because we were now about to combine the families. They came over, everything was normal. I turned the television on, and we watched a movie together. We all talked for a while and then my fiancé and I made our exit into my bedroom.

The kids never paid attention because this had happened many times before. Of course, I knew this wasn't the proper thing to do but "when lust hath conceived, it bringeth forth sin: and sin, when it is finished, bringeth forth death." (James: 1:15) We were there for about an hour and a half when my doorbell rang. I thought: "who could it be at eleven o'clock at night?" I hurried out of the room, passed the kids asleep on the couch and answered the door. There stood my sister. This was not who I wanted to see at this late hour and not while I was in the bedroom with someone, I had no business in the bedroom with. Yes, I was going to church trying to live a saved life. Not really realizing I needed deliverance from "sexual immorality (1 Corinthians 6:18, Hebrews 13:4, 1

A WOMAN WITH CHILDHOOD ISSUES

Thessalonians 4:3-5) I had a lust issue. My fiancé stayed in the bedroom for some time.

My sister stayed so long until he had to come out. She told me she was on her way home and the Lord said: "go by Deb's." When she said that, I knew I was busted. When he came out of the room, she then knew what had taken place. My sister asked him a question which made him mad. She asked: "should a minister be at a single woman's house this late and in her bedroom?" She knew the answer. He never answered. Now, she did not let me escape. The Lord had been dealing with me about this before, but I just ignored His voice once again. Since it was late and the bedroom activity was interrupted, my fiancé, his children and my sister all left. After they left, I put my son to bed, and I decided to lay down on the sofa. I fell asleep and that's when I was shown the lake of fire.

I fell into a deep sleep. In my dream, I saw Jesus glide into my room as though He was on a cloud. He had on a long white robe. I never saw His face or His feet. As I saw Him coming into my room. I sat up in my bed and screamed "FORGIVE ME JESUS!" Because I knew what I had done, I knew He had also seen my antics. He came over to me, placed two of His fingers over my mouth silencing me. WOW - the power He had in just two of His fingers! He then rolled back the wall that was in the room revealing the Lake of Fire written about in Matthew 25:41 to me.

The people in the lake were screaming with high pitched voices, weeping, wailing and gnashing of teeth (Matthew 13:42). There was fire all around their heads. They just kept screaming and screaming with no relief in sight. I knew they were in excruciating pain. I did not recognize anyone. Jesus then rolled the wall back to its original form. I was terrified at what I had seen. He then pointed to me, looked at me and said: "I have called you to do a work, I'm going away, but I'm coming back and I'm coming back for you." (Revelation 22:12). As He made that statement, still pointing at me, He continued: "you'd better get in a hurry! You'd better get in a hurry!" He did not say to me He was coming back for the entire world, He said He was coming back for me. He then put one finger up and said: "I'm going to give you one more chance."

He then gave me a message for a young man I went to school with and glided out of the room still pointing at me saying: "you'd better get in a hurry; you'd better get in a hurry." (Matthew 24:42-51). While still dreaming, I saw myself jump up off the bed and run to my sister's house to tell her what I had witnessed. That's when I woke up. When I did,

A WOMAN WITH CHILDHOOD ISSUES

I was sweating and out of breath from running in my dream.

I did not have to have an interpreter to relay to me what I had experienced. I was so terrified when I woke up, I could not believe I was still alive. I knew Jesus had come to sentence me to the lake of fire. If I had died that night, no one would have known where I went or what happened. I'm just so thankful for being alive and that Jesus gave me another chance to get it right.

I had been told for years that there was a call on my life, but I had made up in my mind that I wasn't going to accept it. To accept it meant I would have to preach. I thought after all the hurt I had seen preachers go through I couldn't do that. I got up to get dressed for work as usual only this time, I was still terrified of the message I received. I went to work and cried all day. I could still hear Jesus' words saying to me: "you'd better get in a hurry; you'd better get in a hurry." I heard that message with impact for months. To this day, I can still see what I saw then so vividly.

I know that whatever the Lord has prepared for you, you will have to do it or face the consequences and we don't know what they may be. Decide today to serve Him as He has called you to do. He will be with you every step of the way.

AS I LOOK BACK

As I look back, I was really playing with my life. I could have lost my life and been burning all these years. I believe there's a heaven, and I sure believe there is a hell. My disobedience could have cost me everything. I often think of all the souls that I would have missed witnessing to if I had died that night. I think of my son who was given to me to be raised in the church, where would he have ended up.

I GET IT

Sometimes, we as women just need to be alone until we heal from our past issues. I had so many issues then and I just swept them under the rug. Ignoring things don't mean they never happened. I know now that every experience we have gone through is designed to teach us something, to build character, to strengthen areas where we are weak, to sharpen, fine tune and refine those things that we will need to help someone else. We have scars and scar tissue. We have holes in our hearts and in our souls, but if we are willing to trust God to heal it all – we will receive His power and we will make it through – issues and all.

THERE IS THE SPIRIT

I will never forget that "lake" experience. I made a promise to God that I would share my story wherever I go and with whomever He says, even if people don't believe me. My fornication stopped and I truly gave my heart to the Lord in all sincerity. Yes, the gentleman and I did marry. I am so grateful that He did not sentence me to "the lake of fire" that night because I know I would have been burning for over twenty-eight years. I am now running for my life, sharing the Gospel of Jesus Christ. He is my all in all. I love Him with all my heart, mind and soul.

Issue 7

MY JOURNEY CONTINUES, MY LIFE TODAY!

After all I've been through, I STILL LOVE the Lord with all my heart, mind and soul. I am saved - for real - and committed to God. Committed to serving Him and Him alone. I've had a lot of bumps and bruises along the way, but I wouldn't erase anything from my journey right now. I have gone through a lot, but God has brought me through. I don't look like what I've been through, yet I praise the Lord because without a test, there will be no testimony. How will people know what God can do if I don't share my story? Some things took longer to understand than I had hoped but nevertheless, God has been good to me.

I remember, about 2009, the Lord revealed something to me that I never knew. To be honest, it never crossed my mind. Even though I thought I was smart and knew everything about myself, He revealed something that brought me to tears. I was sitting watching television one evening, and He spoke to me, I remember like it was yesterday. He said: "Do you remember these stories, "**The woman with the issue of blood**," **(Matthew 9:20-22)** "**The woman caught in adultery**" **(John 7:53-8:11)** and "**The woman at the well" (John 4:4-42**)?" He continued: "You were all three of those women in one body." My God, tears filled my eyes. I thought about those women and I said: "Lord it's a wonder I'm still in my right mind."

I cried for days, wondering how I was still living after being all three of those women in one body. When I read each story, I wondered how they survived. Then to be told by the Lord Himself, that I was them. Looking back over my life, I could identify with each woman. The abortion, with the hemorrhaging that almost took my life, husband coming home finding another man running out of the house, and having three husbands, that God never gave me. I know now, that the hand of God has been on my life, all my life. I can now say to God, thank you for choosing me for Your use.

I'm not any more special than the rest of my siblings. I know God chose me from my mother's womb. I was picked out to be picked on and chosen to suffer. After all these years, as I toiled with writing this book, I am now able to say, "Thank You, Jesus!" In 2016, the Lord spoke to me and told me He was moving me back to Arizona. I knew it was the voice of the Lord because I got too excited. Remember, I had purposed in my heart that I would never visit, let alone move back to the place where I experienced so much pain.

I remember about a year and a half before the Lord spoke that to me, one of the ministers from the church I attended said: "Sister Debbie, God is going to send you back to your Egypt." I looked at him because he had never heard my testimony, he didn't know Tucson was my "Egypt". When he spoke it, I knew it was God, but at that time God knew I wasn't ready to accept that assignment. Why would God send me back there? I just knew God wouldn't take me back to the place of my pain. But I was wrong, God will take you back for several reasons.

There are times when we think we're healed in different areas and we are so far from it. He could be taking us back to be a witness for Him to those who knew our old lives and now we can be that witness we could not have been if we would had stayed. I know now that if I would have stayed there, I would have been dead because of the life I lived. God pulled me out to save me so that others would be saved through my life story. I am now free to be that witness for the Lord Jesus Christ. I have had several opportunities to share my story. I am now ready to live all I know for Him. I commit my whole life to Him.

I left my mom (one of my best friends), sisters, brothers, children, grandchildren, and a host of friends to go back to where God needed me. **Luke 14:33** says: "so likewise, whosoever he be of you that forsakes not all that he hath, he cannot be my disciple." Also, **Matthew 19:29** says: "and everyone that hath forsaken houses, or brethren, or sisters, or father, or mother, or wife, or children, or lands for my name's sake, shall receive a hundredfold, and shall inherit everlasting life."

After everything I've gone through, I really want eternal life. I know that the Lord only spared my life to do His Will and not mine. Before I left Oregon, He even gave me the name of the church He wanted me to attend. I love the song, "I Surrender All." It has more meaning to me today than it ever has. Yes, I surrender all to the Lord, for Him to use me as He pleases. I am willing to do whatever He says to do, go wherever He says to go, say whatever He tells me to say. I now accept the assignment on my life. I know that He will take loving care of me. He always has. Even when I didn't know who He was, He was there all the time. This has been my FAITH journey.

I miss my family, but I love God more. I know that I don't have a long time to do what I've been called to do. And I have wasted so much time. "And that, knowing the time, that now it is high time to awake out of sleep: for now, is our salvation nearer than when we believed." **(Romans 13:11)**. The Lord has already let me know that He will not allow me to live for Satan again and live. He will not allow me to willfully sin and live. His Love is so deep, so unexplainable. I love Him with everything that's within me. No, I don't understand everything that I even go through now, but I know that if God brought me to it, He will bring me through it. I trust Him totally without reservation. I owe Him my very life. I will never forget what He's done for me. I'll never forget how He set me free. No Never.

AS I LOOK BACK

There are so many things I've experienced; I can honestly say today that I wouldn't want to experience anything I've been through, again. One good thing about it all is I went through it and I didn't get stuck in any of it. I do regret some things. Adopting my son is not one of them, I learned genuine love on a different level being his mother. I didn't always get it right. I may have had some failures; but he is a wonderful blessing. And, he has blessed my life with a daughter-in-law and two beautiful grandchildren.

THERE IS THE SPIRIT, I GET IT – NOW...

Throughout my life I have had to go back and make some apologies. So many people got hurt through many decisions that I made. I'm so glad before my dad and my aunt passed, we had a chance to discuss the abortion. I truly forgave them because at that time they did what they thought was right by me. My mom, well she is the best! We have an awesome relationship. My mom is my best friend. It feels good to be able to share every and anything with her. I will share things my siblings won't share. She has been my rock. Just knowing some of the things she's endured has helped me to endure. I'm am so thankful to the Lord that I got the chance to know my mom in an authentic way.

I pray that my life story has helped someone to understand why you've gone through what you've gone through. God can bring you out of anything if you just trust Him and believe in His Son, Jesus Christ. He loves you with an everlasting love and He always will. There's nothing you've been through, nothing you're going through, and nothing you will go through that He won't go through with you if you will only surrender your life to Him.

May God ever Bless and keep you in His care.

www.ingramcontent.com/pod-product-compliance
Lightning Source LLC
LaVergne TN
LVHW021408080426
835508LV00020B/2502